LET'S MAKE & PLAY

Teddy Bear DOCTOR

Be a Vet & Fix the Boo-Boos of Your Favorite Stuffed Animals

Deanna F. Cook

Storey Publishing

CONTENTS

Let's Play Vet!

Do you have a feverish stuffed snake? A plush puppy with a sore paw? Teddy Bear Doctor to the rescue!

In this book, you'll find everything you need to open up your very own pretend vet clinic to heal the ouchies of your fuzzy friends. You'll learn how to bandage wounds on a stuffed kitty, listen to a teddy bear's heartbeat, and look at X-rays to see if your favorite toy dog has a broken leg. Make your own vet equipment and check out the pages at the back of the book to find all kinds of stickers, signs, and other fun things to play with.

Daisy's tummy feels much better now!

Chapter 1

OPEN
Your Vet Practice!

ARE YOU READY TO PLAY PET VET WITH YOUR FUZZY PATIENTS? Start by dressing up as a real vet. You can make a lab coat out of an old T-shirt, craft a pair of glasses with pipe cleaners, and cut out a nurse's hat and headlamp from the pages in the back of the book. Turn a small box into a case for your homemade stethoscope, thermometer, syringe, and other doctor supplies you collect around the house.

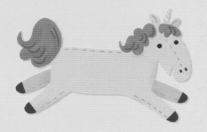

Soon you'll be ready for patients!

T-Shirt Lab Coat

WHAT YOU NEED

- ★ **Large white T-shirt**
- ★ **Scissors**
- ★ **Double-sided tape**

★ **Button stickers**

★ **Arm badge sticker**

★ **Name tag sticker**

VETERINARIAN

Ask the Vet
WEARING SCRUBS

Q *Why do real vets wear lab coats and scrubs?*

A Because they get dirty on the job and need clothes that are easy to clean and change. Their patients may have muddy paws and they often shed fur. An injured animal may be bleeding. When they are sick or nervous, pets sometimes pee, poop, or even vomit. Vets need clean scrubs every day.

What You Do

1. Ask a grown-up to help you cut the front of the T-shirt down the middle.

2. Fold the cut edges back to form lapels, and tape them in place with the double-sided tape.

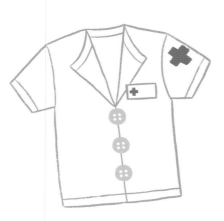

3. Add the button stickers and an arm badge from the back of the book.

4. Fill out the name tag with your name. Stick it on the lab coat.

5. Use double-sided tape to keep the coat closed.

Now you look like a real veterinarian!

Find It at Home
COMPLETE THE LOOK!

You might be able to find these items by looking around the house. If not, they are easy to find at a thrift store or dollar store.

Scrubs. Wear some blue pajama bottoms or long johns with a matching T-shirt under your lab coat to complete your outfit.

Face mask. If you don't have a face mask or dust mask, you can buy one at a pharmacy or hardware store. Or the next time you have an appointment with your doctor or dentist, ask if you can have one to take home.

Exam gloves. These thin gloves can be found at your local pharmacy.

Surgical cap. Use a shower cap! Maybe someone can bring you one from a hotel.

Headlamp

★ **Craft scissors**

★ **Tape and paper clips**

★ **Headlamp template**

What You Do

1. Find the **headlamp template** in the back of the book and tear out along the perforations. Trim off any remaining white.

2. Tape the ends of the two strips together to make a longer headpiece. Wrap it around your head to get the right fit, then tape or clip it into place.

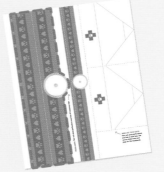

Ask the Vet
LOOK CLOSELY

Q *How do vets examine pets up close?*

A Vets can use a headlamp or magnifying glasses to take a good close look for things like rashes hidden under fur, fleas or other tiny bugs, or small cuts and scratches. They might also use them during surgery to help them see what they're doing.

Eye see you! Examine cuts and scratches up close with a magnifying glass.

Doctor Glasses

What You Do

1. Twist the ends of a pipe cleaner together to make a circle.

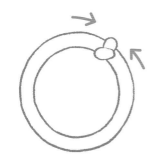

2. Twist the circle to make a figure eight. This forms the frames that rest on your nose.

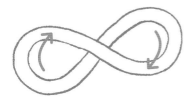

3. Cut a second pipe cleaner in half (ask a grown-up for help). Twist one end of each half to each side of the figure eight.

4. Try them on for size, bending the ends to fit over your ears.

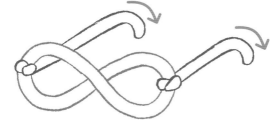

You can make a tiny pair of glasses for a stuffed animal using just one pipe cleaner. Cut it in half and use one half to make the frames. Cut the remaining piece in half again to make the earpieces.

Vet Tech Hat

WHAT YOU NEED

★ Scissors
★ Double-sided tape or glue
★ Small paper clips
★ Vet tech hat template

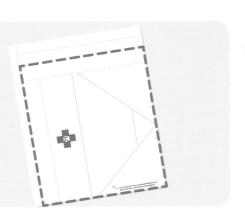

What You Do

1. Find the **vet tech hat template** in the back of the book. Tear out along the perforations to make the main part of the hat and two strips for the headband.

2. With the red cross facing up, fold down the top two corners of the hat along the solid blue line to make a triangle.

3. Fold down the tip of the triangle as shown. Tape or glue the tip to the back of the hat.

4. Flip the hat over, and tape or glue the headband ends to the front of the hat as shown.

5. Fold up the brim so that the red cross is showing. Tape or glue the brim in place.

6. Try on the hat. (If you're using glue, let it dry completely first.) Tape or clip the headband ends so the hat fits snugly.

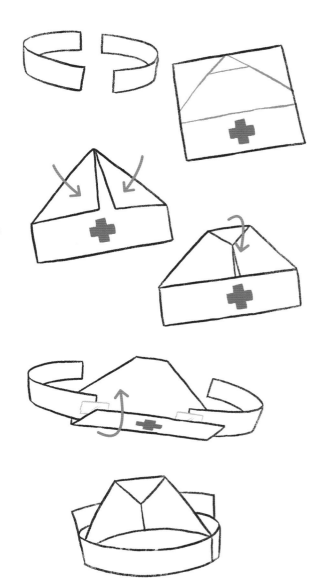

Will I feel better soon?

VETERINARIAN
My name is: MARGAUX

FURRY ASSISTANT

Don't have a friend to play the part of the vet tech? Look in the back of the book for mini hat and headband templates to match yours. Make a smaller hat or headlamp for one of your furry friends and have him be your trusty assistant.

Sam the Siamese Cat will be your vet tech today.

Meet Doctor Dottie!

11

Pipe Cleaner Stethoscope

WHAT YOU NEED

★ 6 pipe cleaners (2 blue, 2 white, 2 red)

★ 1 large button (1 to 2 inches across)

★ 3 plastic bottle caps (1 flip-off type, 1 squeeze-top type, and 1 twist-off type)

★ Glue or glue dots

★ Paw-print sticker

What You Do

1. Twist together one blue and one white pipe cleaner and bend them at the ends as shown. Repeat with the other blue and white pipe cleaners and the two red pipe cleaners.

2. Slip the ends of the blue and white pipe cleaners into the top holes of the button. Slip the end of the red pipe cleaner into the bottom holes. Twist to secure.

3. Glue the button into the bottom of the flip-off cap to secure the short ends of the pipe cleaners in place. Stick the paw-print sticker on the top.

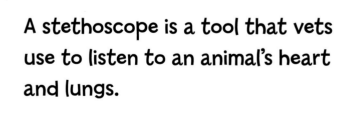

A stethoscope is a tool that vets use to listen to an animal's heart and lungs.

4. Have a grown-up make a hole in the edge of the twist-off cap with a nail. Starting from the outside of the cap, slide the end of the red pipe cleaner into the hole about 1 inch. Untwist the ends, and bend them around the inside of the lid. Glue them into place.

5. Glue the squeeze-top cap on the top of the twist-off cap. Let all the glue dry before using your stethoscope.

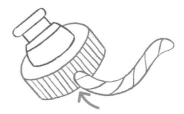

Slip the stethoscope around your ears (not in them) and listen up!

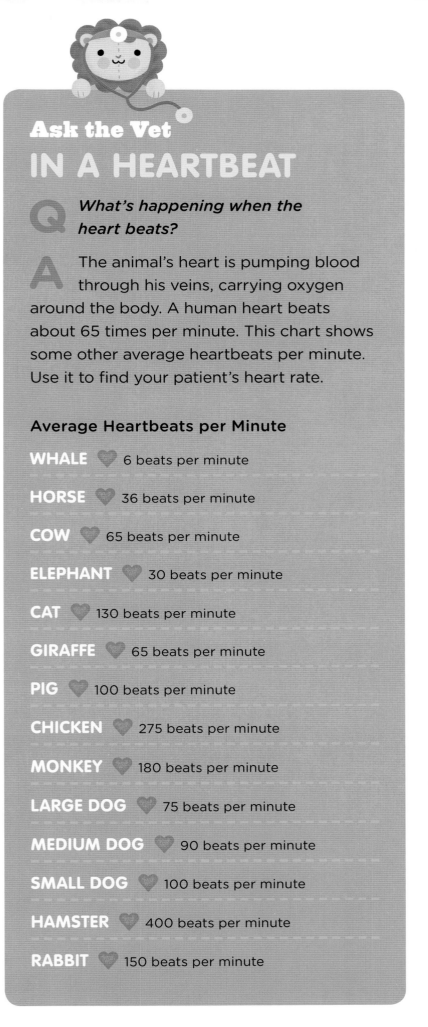

Ask the Vet
IN A HEARTBEAT

Q *What's happening when the heart beats?*

A The animal's heart is pumping blood through his veins, carrying oxygen around the body. A human heart beats about 65 times per minute. This chart shows some other average heartbeats per minute. Use it to find your patient's heart rate.

Average Heartbeats per Minute

WHALE ♥ 6 beats per minute

HORSE ♥ 36 beats per minute

COW ♥ 65 beats per minute

ELEPHANT ♥ 30 beats per minute

CAT ♥ 130 beats per minute

GIRAFFE ♥ 65 beats per minute

PIG ♥ 100 beats per minute

CHICKEN ♥ 275 beats per minute

MONKEY ♥ 180 beats per minute

LARGE DOG ♥ 75 beats per minute

MEDIUM DOG ♥ 90 beats per minute

SMALL DOG ♥ 100 beats per minute

HAMSTER ♥ 400 beats per minute

RABBIT ♥ 150 beats per minute

Pencil Thermometer

WHAT YOU NEED

* ★ Pencil
* ★ Pencil-top eraser
* ★ Thermometer sticker

What You Do

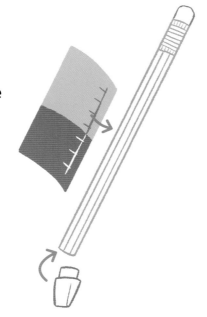

1. Find the **thermometer sticker** in the back of the book. Carefully wrap it around the pencil.

2. Cover the pencil tip with the eraser.

Ask the Vet
TAKING A TEMP

Q *Why is temperature important?*

A For humans, a normal temperature is 98.6°F (37°C). For cats and dogs, a normal temperature is a little higher: between 99.5°F (37.5°C) and 102.5°F (39°C).

If their temperature runs higher, they may have an infection or heatstroke. If their temperature is low, they could be very ill.

Vets can bring a temperature down with a cool bath or medicine. They warm their patients up with snuggle disks (hot water bottles) and blankets.

Is your fuzzy fox feeling feverish? Check his temperature to find out!

Eye & Ear Scope

WHAT YOU NEED

* 1 pipe cleaner
* Cone-shaped plastic cap (from mustard or honey bottle)
* Electrical or duct tape
* Thick felt-tip marker with cap
* Scissors

Take a close look at your patient's eyes and ears with a homemade ophthalmoscope (pronounced off-THAL-muh-scope).

What You Do

1. Wrap the pipe cleaner tightly around the open nozzle of the cap, creating one longer end and one shorter end.

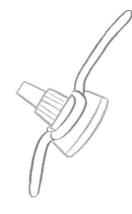

2. Fold the longer end into the underside of the cap and tape it down.

3. Tape the pipe cleaner ends securely to the marker, making sure the cap is snug against the top of the marker. Trim off the ends of the pipe cleaner if necessary.

You can also use this instrument to check stuffy noses and sore throats.

Squirt Bottle Syringe

* ★ **Pump from a soap or lotion dispenser**
* ★ **Cleaned out lip balm tube**
* ★ **Twist top from a glue container**
* ★ **Glue or glue gun**
* ★ **Syringe sticker**

What You Do

1. Wash and dry all the recyclables.

To remove the lip balm from the tube, ask a grown-up to use pliers to take it apart.

2. Slip the bottom of the pump dispenser into the plastic tube.

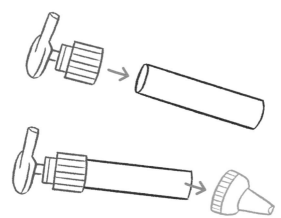

3. Slide the glue top onto the tip of the pump dispenser top as shown. Glue it in place.

4. Wrap the sticker around the lip balm tube.

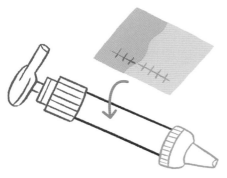

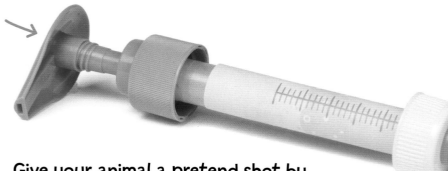

Give your animal a pretend shot by pressing the top of the syringe.

Role Play
BEDSIDE MANNER

Animals get shots at their checkup appointments just like kids. The shots protect them from diseases. You might be a little nervous about getting shots yourself. When you give your stuffed animals a shot, talk kindly to them so they relax.

SAY

"You're being such a good patient."

"Great job!"

"You are so brave."

When you're done, put on a Band-Aid and give them a sticker.

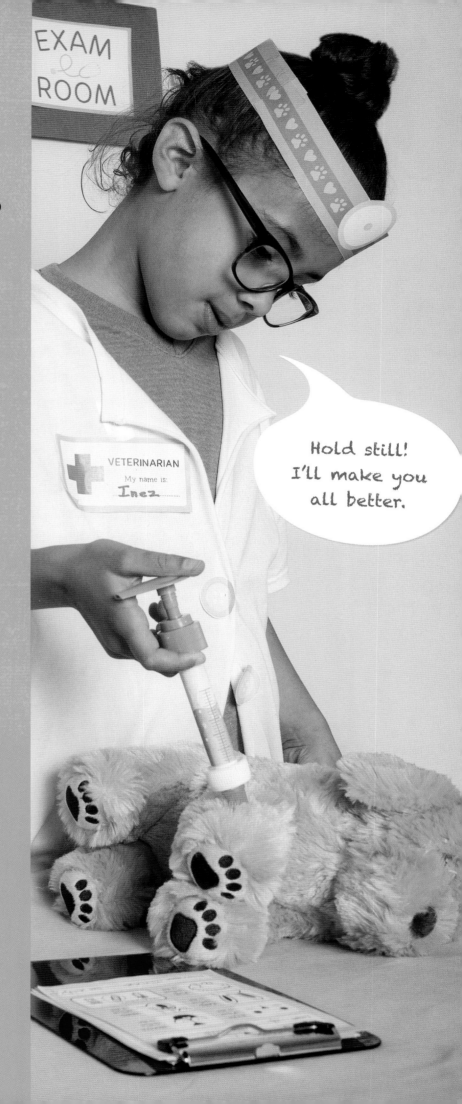

Pet Vet Kit

WHAT YOU NEED

* Box with a hinged lid
* Hole punch
* 12-inch length of ribbon
* Colored paper
* Tape or glue
* Pet Vet Kit sticker

What You Do

1. Ask a grown-up to help you make two holes in the box using a hole punch.

2. To make the handle, knot one end of the ribbon. Thread the other end through the hole, then down through the second hole. Knot the second end.

3. Cut a piece of colored paper to fit the top of the box, and tape or glue it in place. Find the **Pet Vet Kit sticker** in the back of the book, and stick it on the colored paper.

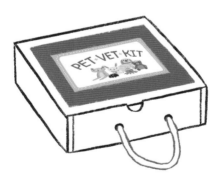

Store all your vet tools in your new kit!

COMPLETE YOUR VET KIT

Look for these items from around your house. Add them to your vet kit, and you'll be ready for business. If you have a toy doctor kit already, you can use those supplies for your animal patients as well.

- ☐ Tweezers
- ☐ Elastic bandages
- ☐ Wooden craft sticks for tongue depressors
- ☐ Eyedroppers
- ☐ Magnifying glass
- ☐ Toothbrush
- ☐ Bulb syringe for ears and nose

Chapter 2

Welcome to the WAITING ROOM!

WHEN FUZZY PETS VISIT THE VET, THEY HAVE TO WAIT THEIR TURN, just like people patients do. In this chapter, you'll make a waiting room with chairs, magazines, and even a toy box. Then you'll set up the front desk so you can file important patient records.

Invite some friends to join in the fun. One person can take a seat behind the desk and play office manager. Other friends can bring in their pets to be seen. It's fun to switch around and play different parts.

Take a seat, and the doctor will be with you shortly!

Waiting Room

WHAT YOU NEED

★ Chairs and a small table

★ Magazines and books

★ Box for toys

★ Colored paper

★ Tape or glue

★ Toy box sticker

> Toy Box

★ Waiting Room sign

> This way to the
> **WAITING ROOM**
> Please sign in at the front desk

★ Veterinarian Certificate sticker

> **PET VET UNIVERSITY**
> hereby declares that:
> Dr. _____
> has earned the title of
> Certified Pet Veterinarian

★ Office Hours sign

> **OFFICE HOURS**
> Monday through Friday
> 9 AM - 5 PM

★ Open/Closed sign

> **OPEN**
> Please Come In!
> FRONT

> Sorry, We're
> **CLOSED**
> BACK

What You Do

1. Set up a row of chairs for the seating area. Put the table near the chairs. Set the magazines and books on the table.

2. Stick the **Toy Box sticker** on the box, and fill it with small toys for pets to play with.

3. Tear out the **Waiting Room sign,** and tape it to the door or on a wall.

4. Stick the **Pet Vet certificate** to a piece of colored paper for a frame. Write your name, and tape it on the wall or desk.

5. Tear out the **Office Hours** and the **Open/Closed signs** and hang on the door or the wall.

COME ON IN!

Cut out this sign from the back of the book. Make two holes with a hole punch at the top. String with yarn and hang on a doorknob. Turn to Closed when the day is done.

Pet-Friendly Front Desk

WHAT YOU NEED

- ★ Desk and chair
- ★ 1 piece of colored paper
- ★ Old telephone and keyboard
- ★ Pens and pencils
- ★ Pretend money, calculator, and cash box
- ★ Front Desk sticker — Front ● Desk
- ★ Please Sign In! sticker — PLEASE ◫ SIGN IN!
- ★ Jar with candy dish sticker — Have a Sweet Day!

What You Do

1. Set the desk and chair near the waiting area.

2. Cut the colored paper in half. Fold each piece in half lengthwise. Stick the **Front Desk** and the **Please Sign In! stickers** to the folded pieces of paper. Stand the signs on the desk.

3. Arrange the telephone, keyboard, calculator, pens and pencils, money box, and candy jar on the desk.

Mini Filing Cabinet

WHAT YOU NEED

* ★ 8 sheets of colored paper
* ★ Empty tissue box
* ★ Paper or paint
* ★ ABC tab stickers

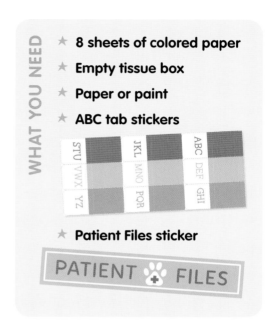

* ★ Patient Files sticker

PATIENT 🐾 FILES

What You Do

1. Make a file folder by folding a piece of paper in half. Add an **ABC tab sticker** at the top edge. Repeat until you have made 9 folders — one for each set of letters.

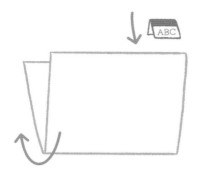

2. Have a grown-up help you cut off the top of a tissue box.

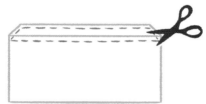

3. Add the **Patient Files sticker** to the front of the box. If you'd like, you can first paint the box or cover it with colored paper.

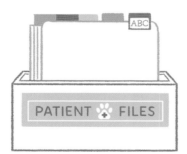

4. Put the folders in alphabetical order in the filing cabinet so you can keep track of patient records.

Now you're ready to start filing!

Role Play
PATIENT CHECK-IN

1. Cut out the **Patient Check-In forms** in the back of the book, and clip them to a small clipboard.

2. When patients arrive, welcome them with a friendly smile. Give pet owners the clipboard and a pencil or pen, and ask them to fill out the sheet.

3. When the vet is ready to see the next patient, hand the form to the doctor so the appointment can start.

Whiskers is not feeling well today.

TAKING CARE OF BUSINESS

What else does a front desk attendant do? Lots of important things!

Answer questions on the phone and talk to pet owners about taking care of their pets.

Pull the patient's folder from the filing cabinet and file the new forms after the appointment is over.

Give pet owners the bill for the visit and take their payments. Offer their pets a treat from the candy dish or a sticker from the toy box.

You can gather small pet toys, collars, and gifts to sell to patients at the front desk.

Schedule appointments for visits, using the **Appointment cards** in the back of the book. Fill in the time on the clock, and circle the type of visit.

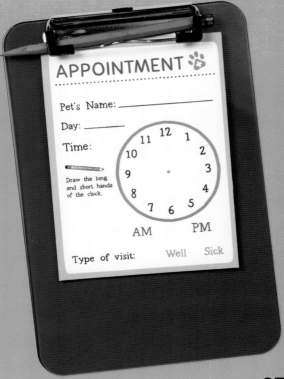

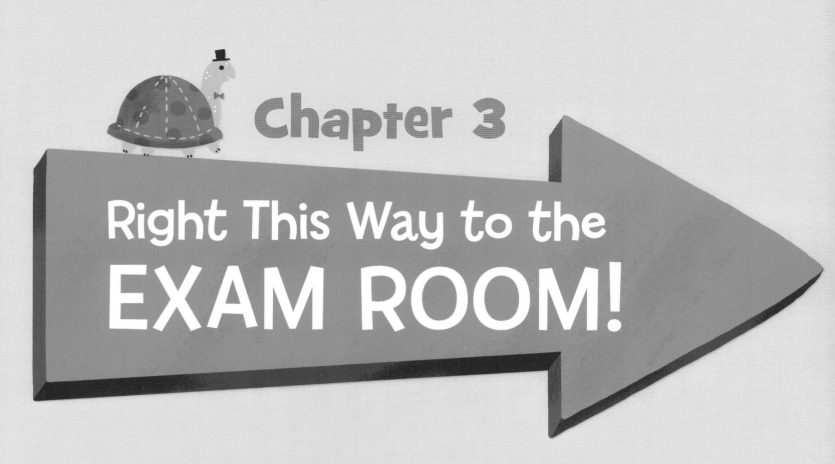

Chapter 3

Right This Way to the EXAM ROOM!

NOW IT'S TIME FOR THE ANIMALS TO SEE THE VET. First you have to set up the exam room and a furry pharmacy for medicines. You'll find special checkup and prescription forms in the back of the book.

Then you'll use your instruments and supplies to examine each of your furry patients. Follow the easy directions for making splints and slings and checking X-rays!

The doctor will see you now!

Exam Room

WHAT YOU NEED

- ★ Table with a blanket or sheet
- ★ Pet Vet Kit (page 18)
- ★ Tray
- ★ Jars of cotton swabs and cotton balls
- ★ Scale
- ★ Tape measure
- ★ Empty bookshelf or another small table
- ★ Small clipboard
- ★ Exam Checklists

- ★ X-rays

- ★ Exam Room sign

- ★ Treat jar sticker

What You Do

1. Set up a small exam table. Top the table with a cozy folded blanket or sheet.

2. Place your vet tools on a tray (the stethoscope, thermometer, and other items from your Pet Vet Kit).

3. Put jars of cotton balls and swabs, the scale, and the tape measure on the bookshelf or second table. That's where the pharmacy will also go (page 38).

4. Tear out the **Exam Checklists** from the back of the book, and clip them onto a small clipboard. Tear out the **X-rays** and put them on the wall or near your other equipment. Tear out and hang up the **Exam Room sign.**

5. Make a treat jar with the label sticker so you can give pets a reward for behaving well during their exams.

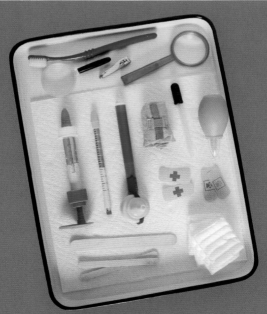

INSTRUMENT TRAY

Having all your instruments laid out on a tray makes it easy to find them while you're examining your patient.

Role Play
TIME FOR A CHECKUP

1. When your patient arrives, place him on the exam table.

2. Use an Exam Checklist from your clipboard to write down all the important information.

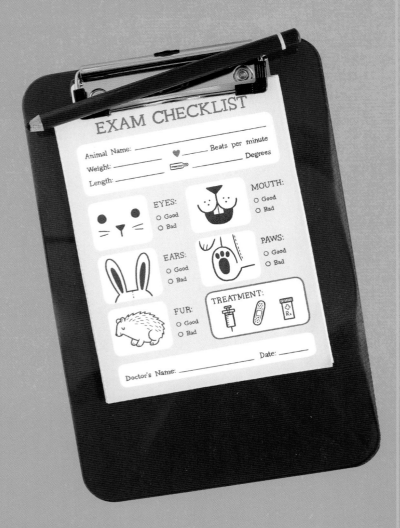

Remember to fill in each patient's name at the top so you can file the form later on.

Weigh her on the scale.

Measure his length with the tape measure.

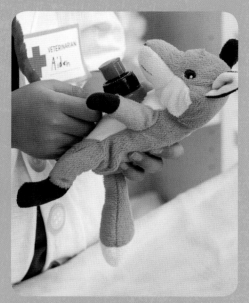

Listen to her heartbeat with your stethoscope. Write down the number of beats per minute.

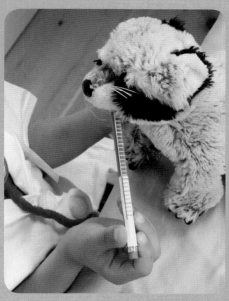

Check her temperature with your thermometer.

Look in her ears and eyes with your ophthalmoscope.

Open your mouth wide and say "Ahhhh..."

Look inside his nose and mouth.

Check his paws and fur. Use your magnifying glass to look closely.

3. Ask the pet owner these questions (and any others you think are important):

 ASK →

How is your pet feeling today?

What is the reason for your visit?

What kind of food does your pet eat? How often?

Any changes in appetite?

Is this an indoor or outdoor pet?

Is your pet acting differently?

Ask the Vet
DOING A CHECKUP

Q *Why does the vet give pets a massage?*

A Vets do an all-over body check to feel for lumps and scratches. They see if there are any "ouchy" spots and check the lymph nodes located in the jaw, armpits, and groin. If those are swollen, the animal may be sick.

Ask the Vet
X-RAY MACHINE

Q *What's the difference between a sprain and a broken bone?*

A If an animal is limping, it might have hurt or sprained some muscles. In that case, rest and some pain medication will do the trick.

But if it's broken a limb, then the vet will put a cast on to hold the bone together while it heals.

Real vets use X-rays to find out if the bone is broken. An X-ray is a special machine that takes pictures of bones inside the body.

Have you ever had to have an X-ray yourself? Then you know it doesn't hurt, but the machine makes a funny noise.

Can you find the two X-rays that show broken bones?

(Find these X-rays at the back of the book.)

Role Play
MAKE IT ALL BETTER

After you diagnose the problem, here's how to make your patients feel better.

PROBLEM	FIX
Scratching and itching	Give the pet some flea medicine.
Itchy, red eyes	Clean the eye with a cotton ball and water. Once the fur dries, put on an eye patch sticker.
Bad breath	Brush the pet's teeth.
Ear infection	Flush the ears out and use a dropper to put in some pretend medicine.
Splinter or thorn in paw	Use tweezers to gently pull it out, clean the area with a cotton ball, and put on a bandage.

What happened to you?

I jumped in a mud puddle full of rocks.

PROBLEM	FIX

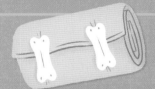

Cut or scrape

 Sometimes vets have to clip the fur to clean and care for the cut, but you don't want to do that on your stuffed animals. You can use a cotton swab or cotton ball, though, to clean the cut before sticking on the bandages.

Sprained leg or paw

Wrap an elastic bandage around the injury.

If you need to keep an injured limb (arm or leg) still while it heals, you can make a sling.

1. Fold two attached sheets of paper towel into thirds.

2. Wrap the middle of the sling twice around the pet's front paw. Tape the ends together behind the patient's neck.

3. Add a bandage sticker to cheer up your fuzzy friend.

Broken limb

Use a wooden craft stick under the bandage to keep the bone straight. You can use a small elastic bandage or fold a paper towel into thirds. Use a red-cross or bandage sticker to keep it in place.

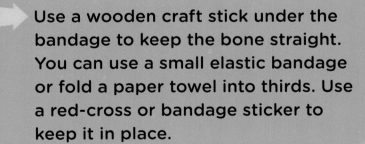

Furry Friend Pharmacy

* Small, clean containers, such as baby food or spice jars, or vitamin or medicine bottles

* Raisins, tiny crackers, sunflower seeds, or other small treats

* Clipboard and pen

* Medicine bottle stickers

* Pet Vet Rx forms

What You Do

1. Stick a **medicine bottle sticker** on each bottle or jar.

2. Fill the bottles with small treats for pills. You can also used different types of dried beans. Or you can crumple up tiny pieces of colored construction paper into balls.

3. Cut out the **Pet Vet Rx forms** in the back of the book, and clip them to a small clipboard or file them in a box.

VERY IMPORTANT: Remember that you are making pretend medicine. In real life, some pills look like candy, so you should never eat anything from a bottle without an adult's permission, even a vitamin pill.

HOME CARE

After you finish the exam, fill out the **Pet Vet Rx form** with instructions for the pet owner.

→ Give the pet owner the form with the official homecare instructions (rest indoors, eat soft foods, and other orders).

→ Give the patient some medicine, if needed.

→ Remember to sign your name at the bottom!

I hope those pills taste like bacon!

Rx is a symbol that stands for "prescription," and it's used to show that a patient needs some medication.

Chapter 4

Rest Up in the RECOVERY ROOM

DOES THE SICK PET NEED TO STAY OVERNIGHT IN THE HOSPITAL? Set up an area for quiet recoveries with the tips in this chapter. Make cozy animal cages from cardboard boxes, and stack them together on a shelf. Fill out an ID tag for each patient. Set up an injured pet with a lampshade collar to protect stitches and cuts. When the pets are ready to go home, send them on their way with Get-Well-Soon stickers!

Here's to a speedy recovery!

RECOVERY ROOM

Patient's Name:
Fluffernutter

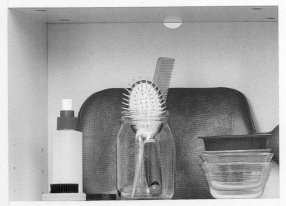
Treats!

STAR PATIENT

Patient's Name:
Sid Snake

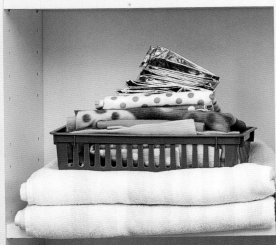

Patient's Name:
Harry

42

Recovery Room

WHAT YOU NEED

- ★ Colored paper
- ★ Cardboard cages (see next page)
- ★ Shelves or benches for cages and supplies
- ★ Supplies (look for these items around the house):
  - Brush
  - Bowls
  - Nail clippers
  - Hourglass timer
  - Hot water bottle
  - Basin or large plastic bowl (for pretend baths)
  - Empty shampoo bottles
  - Small blankets and towels
- ★ Recovery room sign

RECOVERY ROOM

What You Do

1. Make some cardboard cages for your patients.

2. Set the cages on shelves or benches.

3. Arrange your supplies on a shelf or bench in a corner.

4. Tear out the **Recovery Room sign,** and tape it to the door or on a wall.

This is a nice cozy place for me to get better.

43

Cardboard Cages

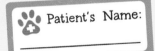
What You Do

1. Have a grown-up cut a large opening on one side of each box. Cut a flap door on one end of the cage that can open and close. Add a duct tape tab to the door for easy opening.

2. Cut a bunch of pieces of yarn into pieces a little bit longer than the opening of the box.

3. Tape pieces of yarn or string from the top of the opening to the bottom, as shown, to look like cage bars. Or leave the box open without bars. Close the top of the box, and tape it shut.

4. Put a blanket or pillow in each cage to make it warm and cozy. Write each pet's name on an ID sticker, and put it on the cage when you tuck them in.

Now you're ready to take care of some sick pets!

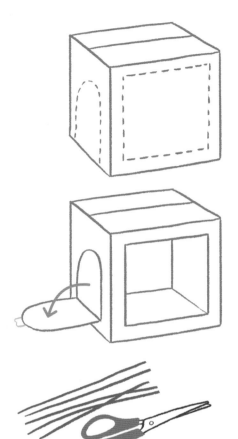

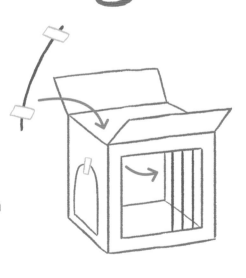

Find It at Home
COZY CAGES

Make the Cardboard Cages nice and comfy for the sick stuffed animals. Look around the house for these items:

Blankets: Line the cages with small towels, doll blankets, or pieces of felt or fleece.

Mini bowls: Fill with water — not too full!

Pet food: Use mini crackers or cookies.

Animal toys: Find some pom-poms or small pet toys.

Pillows: Make them yourself with cotton batting and fabric.

Who-ooo put me in here?

Wheelchair

WHAT YOU NEED

* 1 small rectangular box (a tissue box works)
* Scissors
* Acrylic paint and brushes or markers
* Cardboard scraps for the wheels
* Glue or glue dots
* 2 pipe cleaners
* Tape
* 2 large back wheel stickers

* 2 small front wheel stickers

What You Do

1. Have a grown-up help you cut out the box to make the seat of the wheelchair as shown by the dotted lines.

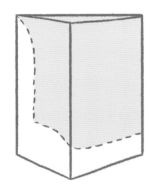

2. If you want, paint the wheelchair or decorate it with markers and stickers.

3. Stick the wheel stickers carefully on the cardboard scraps, and cut around them to make the wheels. Glue them to the side of the box as shown.

4. To make the wheelchair handles, bend the pipe cleaners in half to make a loop. Tape the open ends of each one to the back of the wheelchair, with the loops sticking up. Bend the loops down slightly as shown.

No more monkeying around: stay off your feet.
VETERINARIAN
I promise!

Animal ID Collars

WHAT YOU NEED

* ★ **Scissors**
* ★ **Pen**
* ★ **Tape**
* ★ **Animal ID collars**

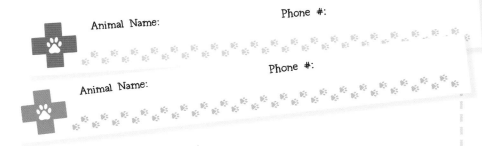

Ask the Vet
COLLAR CONTROL

Q *Why do pets need identification?*

A It's important to have a name, address, and phone number written on the collar of your real pets in case they get lost. Vet assistants remind pet owners to have their pets wear these at all times. Does your real pet have one?

What You Do

1. Find the **animal ID collars** in the back of the book, and cut out along the dotted lines.

2. Fill out the identification information (the pet's name and the owner's phone number).

3. Tape the collar around the patient's neck.

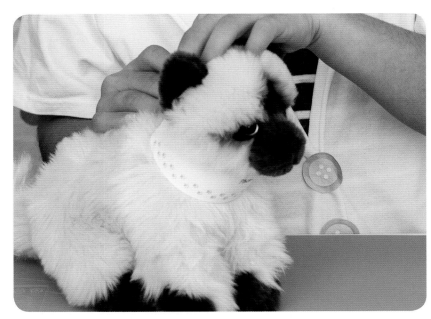

Keep track of your patients with these animal ID collars. ID stands for identification.

Lampshade Collar

★ **Scissors**

★ **Tape**

★ **Lampshade collar**

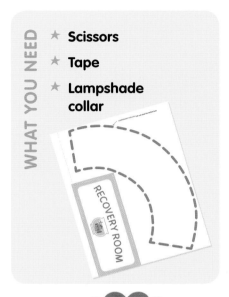

What You Do

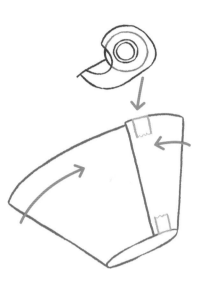

1. Find the **lampshade collar template** in the back of the book, and cut it out along the dotted lines.

2. Wrap it around the pet's head as shown.

3. Tape it in place so it fits snugly.

Ask the Vet
WHAT KIND OF COLLAR IS THAT?

Q *Why do pets sometimes have to wear those funny big collars?*

A When animals have stitches or a sore spot on their skin, they sometimes bite, scratch, or lick it to feel better. But they'll heal faster if you put them in a lampshade collar to protect their boo-boos from too much attention. These are also called Elizabethan collars (or just E-collars).

Role Play
HELPING THEM HEAL

Pretend you are an overnight vet assistant and it's your job to care for the animals. Here are some things you can do:

Fill water bowls and food bowls. Feed them by hand if they need help.

Zzzzz.....

Keep the room quiet. Make the animals comfortable so they can get a good night's sleep.

Take the animals out of their cages, and pet them to comfort them.

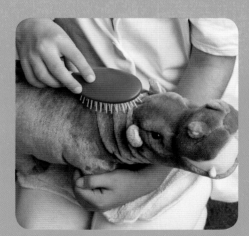

Brush their fur, and clip their nails.

Check the temperature of sick pets.

Give them a pretend bath in a basin.

50

Dedicated to my sister Dr. Hillary Cook, a real veterinarian

The mission of Storey Publishing is to serve our customers by publishing practical information that encourages personal independence in harmony with the environment

Edited by Lisa H. Hiley
Art direction and book design by Jessica Armstrong

Cover photography by © Julie Bidwell, except for Pet Vet Kit (back) by Mars Vilaubi
Interior photography by © Julie Bidwell, except for pages: 1, 8 (top), 9, 10 12, 15 (bottom), 16, 18, 19, 27 (bottom right), 36 (bottom), 37 (middle and bottom), and 46 by Mars Vilaubi
Photo styling by Deanna F. Cook
Craft styling by Maryellen Sullivan
Illustrations by Alyssa Nassner

© 2015 Deanna F. Cook

Storey books are available for special premium and promotional uses and for customized editions. For further information, please call 1-800-793-9396.

Storey Publishing
210 MASS MoCA Way
North Adams, MA 01247
www.storey.com

Printed in China by R.R. Donnelley
10   9   8   7   6   5   4   3   2   1

Library of Congress Cataloging-in-Publication Data on file

THANK YOU!

I want to thank all the great kids who modeled in this book with their stuffed animal friends: Aiden, Inez, Malia, Margaux, Sean, Tate, Teagan, Tejas, Wiley, and Zadie! I'd also like to thank Maryellen Sullivan for all her amazing craft ideas and creativity. Thanks to my family for their support, and to Lauren Atkins and Hillary Cook for their real vet insights. Lastly, thanks to the team at Storey for helping me make this beautiful book, especially Jessica Armstrong, Lisa Hiley, and Deborah Balmuth, and our photographer, Julie Bidwell.

OPEN

Please Come In!

OFFICE HOURS

Monday through Friday
9 AM – 5 PM

This way to the

WAITING ROOM

Please sign in at the front desk.

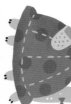

This way to the

WAITING ROOM

Please sign in at the front desk.

Sorry, We're

CLOSED

Open 24 HOURS
for Emergencies

Animal Name: Phone #:

Animal Name: Phone #:

Animal Name: Phone #:

Animal Name: Phone #:

Animal Name: Phone #:

Animal Name: Phone #:

Animal Name: Phone #:

Animal Name: Phone #:

Animal Name: Phone #:

Animal Name: Phone #:

Animal Name: Phone #:

Animal Name: Phone #:

Animal Name: Phone #:

Animal Name: Phone #:

Animal Name: Phone #:

Animal Name: Phone #:

Animal Name: Phone #:

Animal Name: Phone #:

Animal Name: Phone #:

Animal Name: Phone #:

PATIENT CHECK-IN

Name: _____ Date: _____

Owner Name: _____

PET TYPE:

Cat   Bird   Dog   Pig

Bear   Bunny   Hamster   Other

Draw a picture
of what is
bothering your pet.

PATIENT CHECK-IN

Name: _____ Date: _____

Owner Name: _____

PET TYPE:

Cat   Bird   Dog   Pig

Bear   Bunny   Hamster   Other

Draw a picture
of what is
bothering your pet.

PATIENT CHECK-IN

Name: _____ Date: _____

Owner Name: _____

PET TYPE:

Cat   Bird   Dog   Pig

Bear   Bunny   Hamster   Other

Draw a picture
of what is
bothering your pet.

PATIENT CHECK-IN

Name: _____ Date: _____

Owner Name: _____

PET TYPE:

Cat   Bird   Dog   Pig

Bear   Bunny   Hamster   Other

Draw a picture
of what is
bothering your pet.

PATIENT CHECK-IN

Name: _____ Date: _____

Owner Name: _____

PET TYPE:

 Cat   Bird   Dog   Pig

 Bear   Bunny   Hamster   Other

Draw a picture of what is bothering your pet.

PATIENT CHECK-IN

Name: _____ Date: _____

Owner Name: _____

PET TYPE:

 Cat   Bird   Dog   Pig

Bear   Bunny   Hamster   Other

Draw a picture of what is bothering your pet.

PATIENT CHECK-IN

Name: _____ Date: _____

Owner Name: _____

PET TYPE:

 Cat   Bird   Dog   Pig

 Bear   Bunny   Hamster   Other

Draw a picture of what is bothering your pet.

PATIENT CHECK-IN

Name: _____ Date: _____

Owner Name: _____

PET TYPE:

 Cat   Bird   Dog   Pig

Bear   Bunny   Hamster   Other

Draw a picture of what is bothering your pet.

APPOINTMENT 🐾

Pet's Name: _____

Day: _____

Time: _____

Draw the long
and short hands
of the clock.

AM   PM

Type of visit: Well   Sick

APPOINTMENT 🐾

Pet's Name: _____

Day: _____

Time: _____

Draw the long
and short hands
of the clock.

AM   PM

Type of visit: Well   Sick

APPOINTMENT 🐾

Pet's Name: _____

Day: _____

Time: _____

Draw the long
and short hands
of the clock.

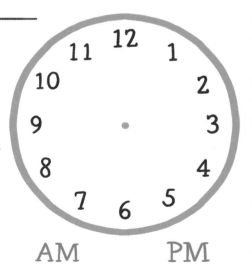

AM   PM

Type of visit: Well   Sick

APPOINTMENT 🐾

Pet's Name: _____

Day: _____

Time: _____

Draw the long
and short hands
of the clock.

AM   PM

Type of visit: Well   Sick

APPOINTMENT 🐾

Pet's Name: _____

Day: _____

Time: _____

Draw the long
and short hands
of the clock.

AM   PM

Type of visit: Well   Sick

APPOINTMENT 🐾

Pet's Name: _____

Day: _____

Time: _____

Draw the long
and short hands
of the clock.

AM   PM

Type of visit: Well · Sick

APPOINTMENT 🐾

Pet's Name: _____

Day: _____

Time: _____

Draw the long
and short hands
of the clock.

AM   PM

Type of visit: Well   Sick

APPOINTMENT 🐾

Pet's Name: _____

Day: _____

Time: _____

Draw the long
and short hands
of the clock.

AM   PM

Type of visit: Well   Sick

EXAM CHECKLIST

Animal Name: _____

Weight: _____  _____ Beats per minute

Length: _____ _____ Degrees

 EYES:
- ○ Good
- ○ Bad

 MOUTH:
- ○ Good
- ○ Bad

 EARS:
- ○ Good
- ○ Bad

 PAWS:
- ○ Good
- ○ Bad

 FUR:
- ○ Good
- ○ Bad

TREATMENT:

Doctor's Name: _____ Date: _____

EXAM CHECKLIST

Animal Name: _____

Weight: _____  _____ Beats per minute

Length: _____ _____ Degrees

 EYES:
- ○ Good
- ○ Bad

MOUTH:
- ○ Good
- ○ Bad

 EARS:
- ○ Good
- ○ Bad

 PAWS:
- ○ Good
- ○ Bad

FUR:
- ○ Good
- ○ Bad

TREATMENT:

Doctor's Name: _____ Date: _____

EXAM CHECKLIST

Animal Name: _____

Weight: _____ ♥ _____ Beats per minute

Length: _____ _____ Degrees

 EYES:
- ○ Good
- ○ Bad

MOUTH:
- ○ Good
- ○ Bad

EARS:
- ○ Good
- ○ Bad

PAWS:
- ○ Good
- ○ Bad

 FUR:
- ○ Good
- ○ Bad

TREATMENT:

Doctor's Name: _____ Date: _____

EXAM CHECKLIST

Animal Name: _____

Weight: _____ ♥ _____ Beats per minute

Length: _____ _____ Degrees

EYES:
- ○ Good
- ○ Bad

 MOUTH:
- ○ Good
- ○ Bad

EARS:
- ○ Good
- ○ Bad

 PAWS:
- ○ Good
- ○ Bad

FUR:
- ○ Good
- ○ Bad

TREATMENT:

Doctor's Name: _____ Date: _____

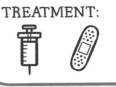

EXAM CHECKLIST

Animal Name: _____

Weight: _____  _____ Beats per minute

Length: _____  _____ Degrees

 **EYES:**
○ Good
○ Bad

 **MOUTH:**
○ Good
○ Bad

 **EARS:**
○ Good
○ Bad

 **PAWS:**
○ Good
○ Bad

 **FUR:**
○ Good
○ Bad

TREATMENT:

Doctor's Name: _____ Date: _____

EXAM CHECKLIST

Animal Name: _____

Weight: _____  _____ Beats per minute

Length: _____  _____ Degrees

EYES:
○ Good
○ Bad

MOUTH:
○ Good
○ Bad

EARS:
○ Good
○ Bad

PAWS:
○ Good
○ Bad

 **FUR:**
○ Good
○ Bad

TREATMENT:

Doctor's Name: _____ Date: _____

EXAM CHECKLIST

Animal Name: _____

Weight: _____  _____ Beats per minute

Length: _____ _____ Degrees

EYES:
○ Good
○ Bad

MOUTH:
○ Good
○ Bad

 **EARS:**
○ Good
○ Bad

PAWS:
○ Good
○ Bad

 **FUR:**
○ Good
○ Bad

TREATMENT:

Doctor's Name: _____ Date: _____

EXAM CHECKLIST

Animal Name: _____

Weight: _____  _____ Beats per minute

Length: _____ _____ Degrees

EYES:
○ Good
○ Bad

MOUTH:
○ Good
○ Bad

 **EARS:**
○ Good
○ Bad

 **PAWS:**
○ Good
○ Bad

 **FUR:**
○ Good
○ Bad

TREATMENT:

Doctor's Name: _____ Date: _____

Pet Vet R̶x̶

Date: _____
Animal's Name:

_____

Homecare:

☐ Rest indoors

☐ Change bandage

☐ Take medicine

☐ Use wheelchair

☐ Eat soft food

☐ Wear collar

X _____

Pet Vet R̶x̶

Date: _____
Animal's Name:

_____

Homecare:

☐ Rest indoors

☐ Change bandage

☐ Take medicine

☐ Use wheelchair

☐ Eat soft food

☐ Wear collar

X _____

Pet Vet R̶x̶

Date: _____
Animal's Name:

_____

Homecare:

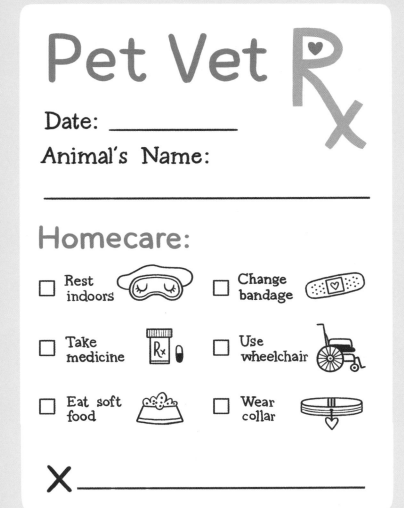

☐ Rest indoors

☐ Change bandage

☐ Take medicine

☐ Use wheelchair

☐ Eat soft food

☐ Wear collar

X _____

Pet Vet R̶x̶

Date: _____
Animal's Name:

_____

Homecare:

☐ Rest indoors

☐ Change bandage

☐ Take medicine

☐ Use wheelchair

☐ Eat soft food

☐ Wear collar

X _____

Pet Vet Rx

Date: _____

Animal's Name:

_____

Homecare:

☐ Rest indoors   ☐ Change bandage

☐ Take medicine   ☐ Use wheelchair

☐ Eat soft food   ☐ Wear collar

X_____

Pet Vet Rx

Date: _____

Animal's Name:

_____

Homecare:

☐ Rest indoors   ☐ Change bandage

☐ Take medicine   ☐ Use wheelchair

☐ Eat soft food   ☐ Wear collar

X_____

Pet Vet Rx

Date: _____

Animal's Name:

_____

Homecare:

☐ Rest indoors 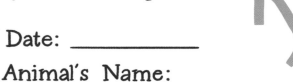   ☐ Change bandage

☐ Take medicine   ☐ Use wheelchair

☐ Eat soft food   ☐ Wear collar

X_____

Pet Vet Rx

Date: _____

Animal's Name:

_____

Homecare:

☐ Rest indoors   ☐ Change bandage

☐ Take medicine   ☐ Use wheelchair

☐ Eat soft food   ☐ Wear collar

X_____

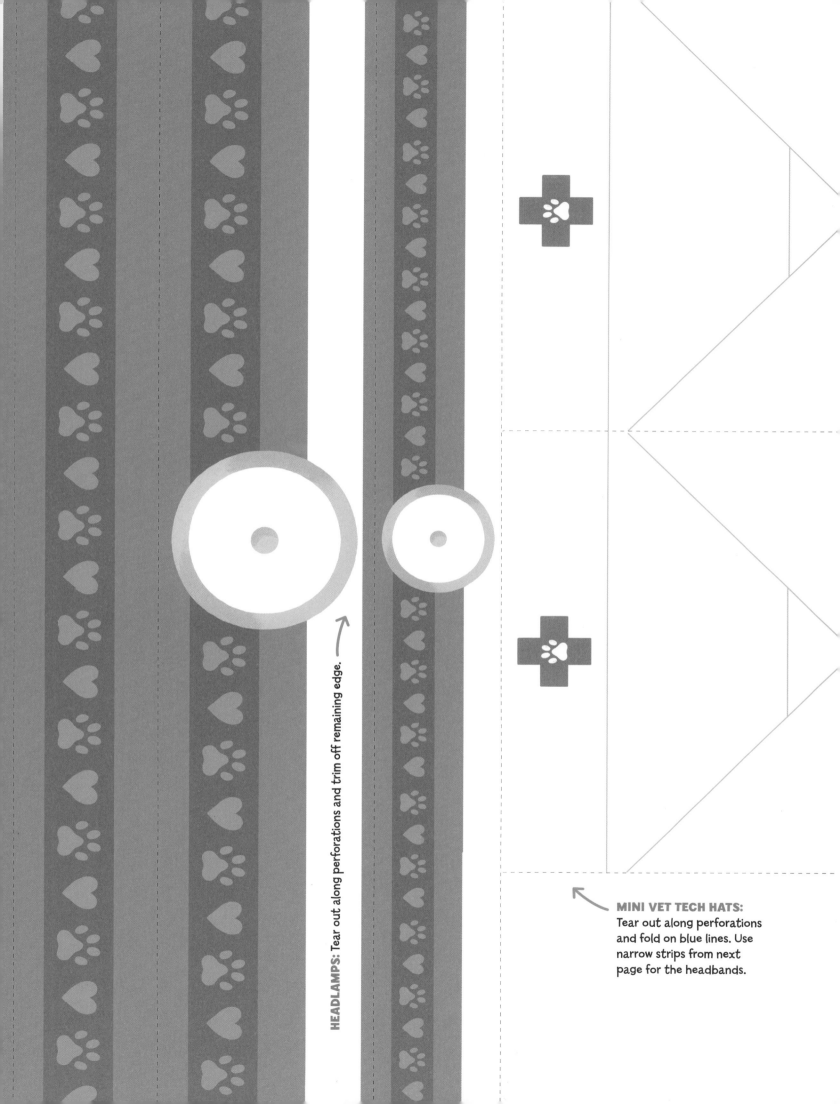

HEADLAMPS: Tear out along perforations and trim off remaining edge.

MINI VET TECH HATS:
Tear out along perforations
and fold on blue lines. Use
narrow strips from next
page for the headbands.

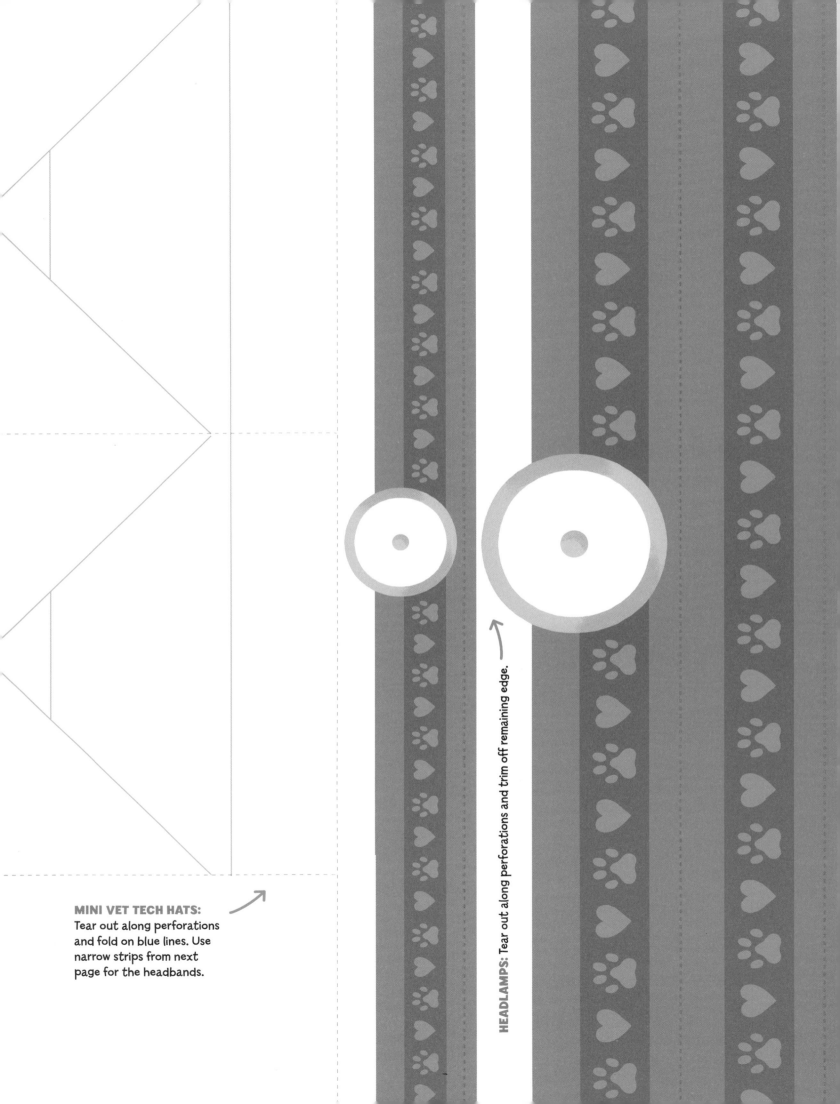

MINI VET TECH HATS:
Tear out along perforations
and fold on blue lines. Use
narrow strips from next
page for the headbands.

HEADLAMPS: Tear out along perforations and trim off remaining edge.

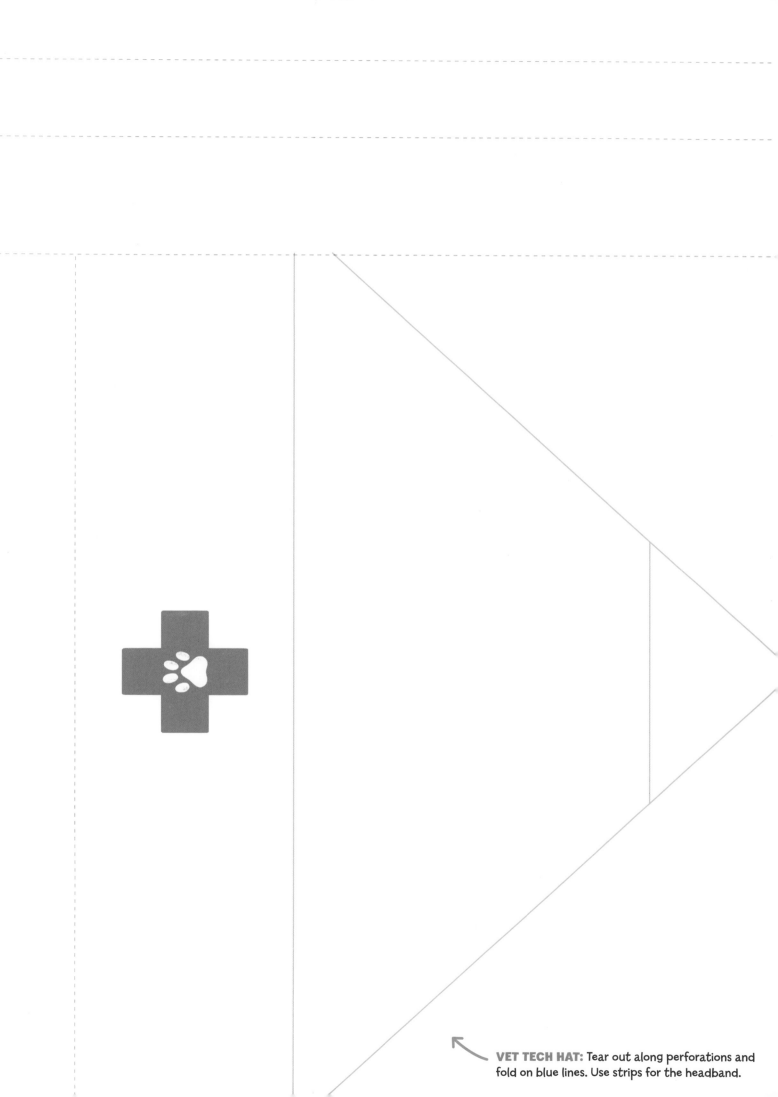

VET TECH HAT: Tear out along perforations and fold on blue lines. Use strips for the headband.

LAMPSHADE COLLAR: Cut out along the dotted lines.

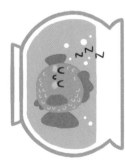

RECOVERY ROOM

RECOVERY ROOM

EXAM ROOM

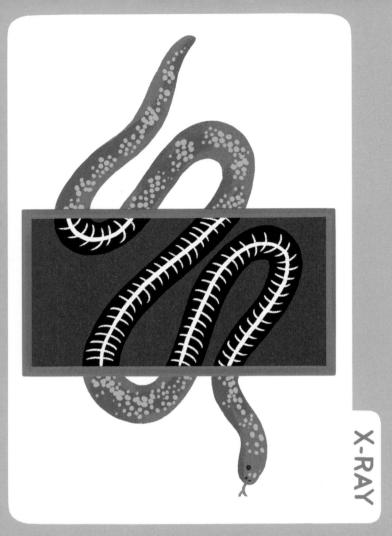

X-RAY

EXAM ROOM

EXAM ROOM

X-RAY

X-RAY

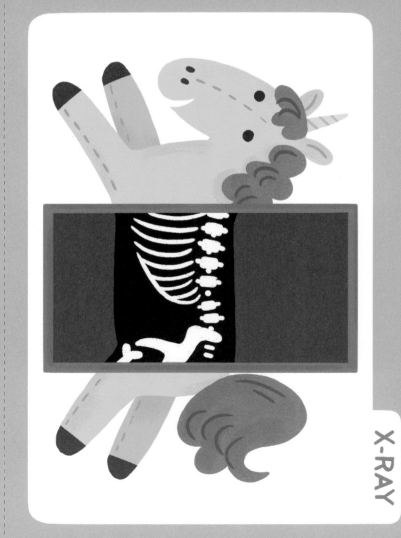

X-RAY

VETERINARIAN

....

VETERINARIAN

....

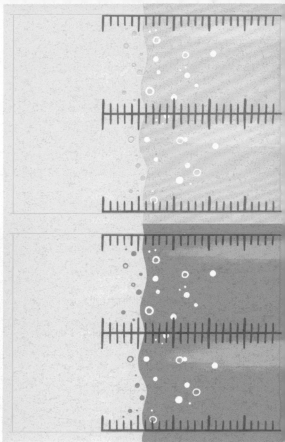

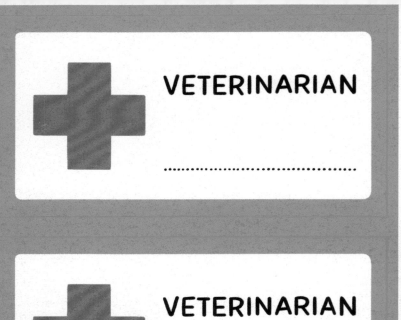

PET + VET + KIT

STU	VWX	YZ

JKL	MNO	PQR

ABC	DEF	GHI

Toy Box

PATIENT FILES

Front Desk

Have a Sweet Day!

PLEASE SIGN IN!

PET VET UNIVERSITY

hereby declares that:

Dr. _____

has earned the title of:

Certified Pet Veterinarian

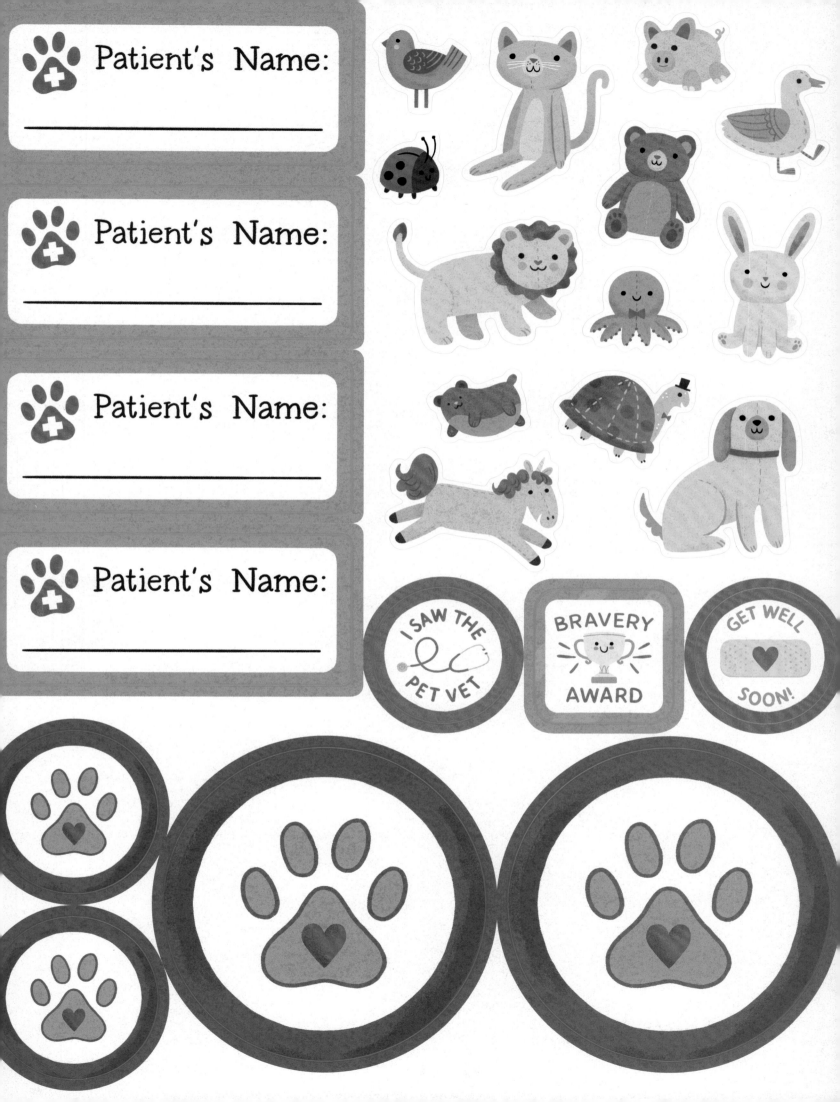

🐾 Patient's Name:
_____

🐾 Patient's Name:
_____

🐾 Patient's Name:
_____

🐾 Patient's Name:
_____

I SAW THE PET VET

BRAVERY AWARD

GET WELL SOON!